T0381204

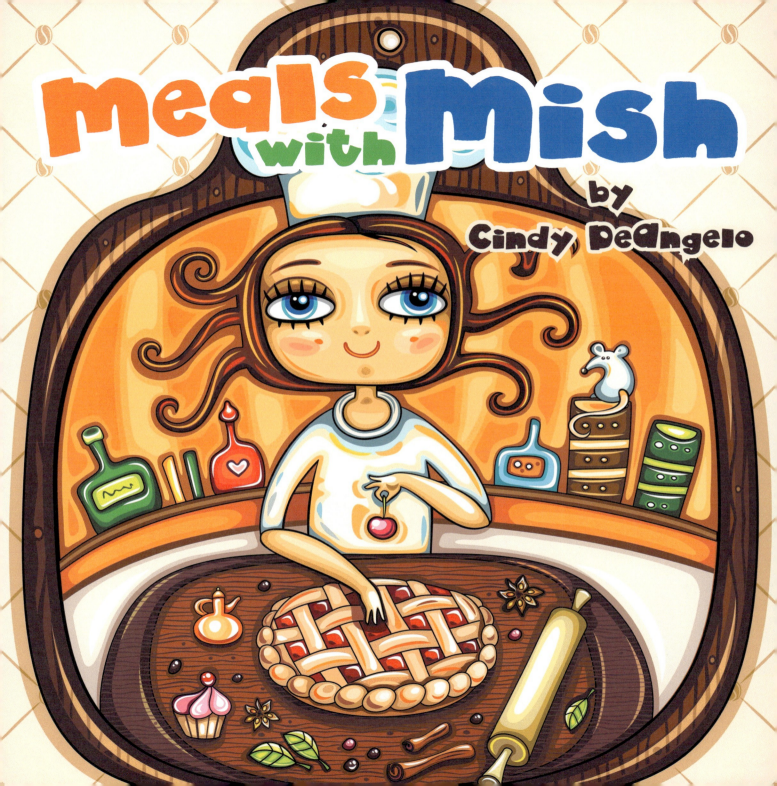

AuthorHouse™
1663 Liberty Drive
Bloomington, IN 47403
www.authorhouse.com
Phone: 1 (800) 839-8640

Because of the dynamic nature of the Internet, any web addresses or links contained in this book may have changed since publication and may no longer be valid. The views expressed in this work are solely those of the author and do not necessarily reflect the views of the publisher, and the publisher hereby disclaims any responsibility for them.

Any people depicted in stock imagery provided by Getty Images are models, and such images are being used for illustrative purposes only.
Certain stock imagery © Getty Images.

This book is printed on acid-free paper.

ISBN: 978-1-5462-3585-9 (sc)

Print information available on the last page.

Published by AuthorHouse   01/28/2020

meals with Mish

Acknowledgement

A "Thank You" goes out to my Mom, the backbone and single unit of the family. Without you we may not be as close as we are especially as sisters and brothers who we not only refer to as siblings but also as BFF's in each other's lives. A big "Tribute" goes out to my Dad the anchor and the strength that taught us love of family.

Special "Thanks" to my husband and partner in bringing his artistic self, spiritual connection and sincere dedication to his music for us to experience and for all to treasure the value of music-making in all of our lives.

"Acknowledgements" go out to the growing number of cousins, nieces, nephews and childhood friends featured in this book who have kept the younger me to recognize the greatest generation and magnificence our family will forever endure!

Last but not least my "Appreciation" and "Gratitude" goes out to my step-children Angela and Alexandria who have added their deepest inspiration to our life in making our family complete.

We hereby acknowledge Marlene Goodman for her artistic talent and drawings of each Caricature and contribution made to this book.

You will all and forever remain in my heart, my mind and in my soul.

Dedications

To my daughter, Michele, who has grown to be my best friend.

When I had started putting this book together I had not realized that girls grow quicker than books. Writing this book has been a great reminder of the joy that you have brought into my life. Whether you're a young girl or a grown-up woman, you will always remain as my little girl. The journey would have never been possible without you and your husband John to whom I refer to as my one and only favorite son-in-law.

BIO

As a native of Chicago and leading author of her first book "Meals with Mish", Cynthia DeAngelo was born in Oak Park, Illinois as Cynthia Gentile. In pursuit of a career in Finance and mother of one they moved to Wheaton, IL where she worked two jobs to overcome the huge obstacles that a single mom encounters trying to raise a daughter with the utmost respect and humility. This book draws on recipes created and prepared for her daughter, Michele (Mish). These culinary creations are light and nutritious while making them fun to eat! From our house to yours we hope you enjoy them as much as we do.

CIAO,
Cindy and Michele

Michele Lee

Table of Contents

Orange French Toast With Orange Butter

INGREDIENTS

- 2 beaten eggs
- 8 thick slices of Italian Bread
- ¼ skim milk
- ¼ cup orange juice
- Dash of cinnamon

DIRECTIONS

1. Beat eggs, milk, orange juice and cinnamon together.
2. Pour into a shallow bowl.
3. Dip each slice of bread into egg mixture
4. Melt some butter or spray pam into a large skillet on medium until hot, Fry until brown on both sides.
5. Top with jelly, jam or Hot Honey Butter

ORANGE BUTTER

INGREDIENTS

- ½ cup softened butter
- 2 tsp. Grated orange rind
- 6 Tbl. Confectioners' sugar

DIRECTIONS

1. Work butter until creamy.
2. Stir in orange rind and confectioners' sugar until smooth.

Makes ⅔ cup

Marvelous Cousin Martina

Martina

Surprise Pannacakes

INGREDIENTS

- 1 cup **Milk**
- 1 cup **pancake mix**
- ½ cup **wheat germ**

- ½ cup **raisins**
- 1 tsp **cinnamon**
- 1 Tbl **salad oil**

DIRECTIONS

1. Heat griddle, grease lightly with **cooking oil**.
2. In a medium size bowl, with rotary beater, beat **milk** with **egg,** add Tbl of **cooking oil** until combined.
3. Stir in pancake mix, wheat germ and raisins.
4. Use ¼ cup of batter for each pannacake.
5. Cook pannacakes until lightly browned about 3 minutes on each side.
6. Serve with butter and syrup or honey butter.

Makes 8 medium pancakes.

Fav of Cousin Frankie

Frankie

Bacon, Egg and Cheesy Scrambler

INGREDIENTS

- 4 **eggs**
- ¼ cup **milk**
- 1 slice of **American cheese**

- 2 slices **uncooked bacon**
- **Salt** and **pepper**
- 2 tablespoons **butter**

DIRECTIONS

1. Break **eggs** into small bowl. Beat with fork until foamy.
2. Add **milk, cheese pieces**, **salt** and **pepper**; mix well.
3. Melt butter in skillet over medium heat.
4. Add **bacon** until medium cooked, add **egg** mixture gradually.
5. Cook until **eggs** are set, stirring frequently with fork.

Amazing Andrea & Michele

Andrea & Michele

Yogurt and Granola Parfait

INGREDIENTS

- ¼ cup **granola**
- ½ cup **plain yogurt**

- 1 tablespoon **maple syrup**

DIRECTIONS

1. Place the **granola** in the bottom of a parfait glass or dish.
2. Spoon the yogurt on top.

Drizzle with **maple syrup**.

Simplified by friend Kelly

Friend Kelly

Easy Croissants with Hot Honey Butter

INGREDIENTS

- 1 8-count tube refrigerated **crescent rolls**
- ⅓ cup **semisweet chocolate chips**

DIRECTIONS

Heat oven to 375° F.

1. Unroll the dough and separate it into 8 triangles.
2. Place about 10 **chocolate chips** on the bottom third of each triangle and
3. Roll the dough up around the chocolate chips.
4. Transfer the **croissants** to a baking sheet (lined with parchment paper, if desired, for easier cleanup).

Bake until golden brown, 12 to 14 minutes.

Serve warm with Hot Honey Butter

HOT HONEY BUTTER

INGREDIENTS

- 1 cup **honey**
- **Cinnamon**
- ¼ cup melted **butter**
- **nutmeg**

1. Warm honey and melted butter
2. Add dash of cinnamon and dash of the nutmeg.
3. Spread on pancakes or toast.

Created for Cousin Luciana

Cousin Luciana

Kiddieland Stuffed Hot Diggity Dogs

INGREDIENTS

- 6 **hotdogs**
- 3 **potatoes**
- 8 oz. grated **cheese**
- ½ stick **butter**
- 6 strips **bacon**
- ¼ cup **milk**

DIRECTIONS

1. Mash and salt **potatoes**
2. Microwave **bacon** crisp and crumble into **mashed potatoes**
3. Split cooked **hotdogs** and stuff with **potatoes**
4. Sprinkle with grated **cheese**

Broil at 400F until brown

Favored by childhood friend Lisa

Friend Lisa

Simple Sloppy Jo Casserole

INGREDIENTS

- 1 pkg (8oz) shell macaroni
- 1 can (8oz) tomato sauce
- 1 envelope Sloppy Joe seasoning mix
- 1 lb ground chuck

- 2 cartons (8oz) creamed cottage cheese
- ½ cup grated Cheddar cheese
- 1 can tomato paste

DIRECTIONS

Pre-heat oven to 350F

1. Cook macaroni as directed; drain.
2. Prepare seasoning mix with ground chuck, tomato paste, tomato sauce, and 1-¼ cups of water, as package directs.
3. In 2-½ quart casserole, layer half the macaroni, half the cottage cheese, and half the meat sauce; repeat.

Bake uncovered, 40-50 minutes or until bubbling.

Liked by Cousin Nick

Cousin Nick

GREAT RECIPE!

Hot Bologna and Cheese Melt

INGREDIENTS

- Two slices of **white bread**
- One slice of **American cheese** for each bread
- One slice of **bologna** for each slice of bread
- One pad of **Butter** or **Margarine** for each slice of bread
- Optional **Mustard** if desired

DIRECTIONS

Preheat oven to 350F degrees

1. On a cookie sheet put the **bread** with **margarine.**
2. On top of that put on one slice of **bologna** and one slice of **cheese**
3. (American cheese).
4. Spread mustard on the top, if desired.

Bake in a heated oven for five to ten minutes until cheese melts.

Innovated Uncle Vince

uncle Vince

Devilish Eggs

INGREDIENTS

- 6 hard-boiled **Eggs**
- ½ teaspoon dry or 1 teaspoon prepared **mustard**
- ¼ teaspoon salt Dash of **pepper**
- 1 to 2 tablespoons finely chopped **butter pickle**

- 3 tablespoons **mayonnaise**
- ½ tablespoon **vinegar**
- ½ teaspoon **Worcestershire sauce**
- **Paprika**

DIRECTIONS

1. Cool hard-boiled **eggs**; shell and halve lengthwise.
2. Carefully lift out **yolks** and place in mixing bowl.
3. Mash with fork and add remaining ingredients **except paprika**
4. Mix until fluffy
5. Fill **egg whites** with yolk mixture

Sprinkle with paprika.

Edibles of Cousin Eric

Cousin Eric

Tortilla Apple-Peanut Butter Wraps

INGREDIENTS

- 1 soft **flour tortilla**
- 1 tablespoon **peanut butter**
- 2 tablespoons **raisins**
- 1 small chopped **sweet apple**

DIRECTIONS

1. Spread **peanut butter** on shell. Sprinkle with **raisins** and **apples**.
2. Roll and enjoy!

Variations: sprinkle with cinnamon or add chopped nuts.

Alluring Cousin Alex

Cousin Alex

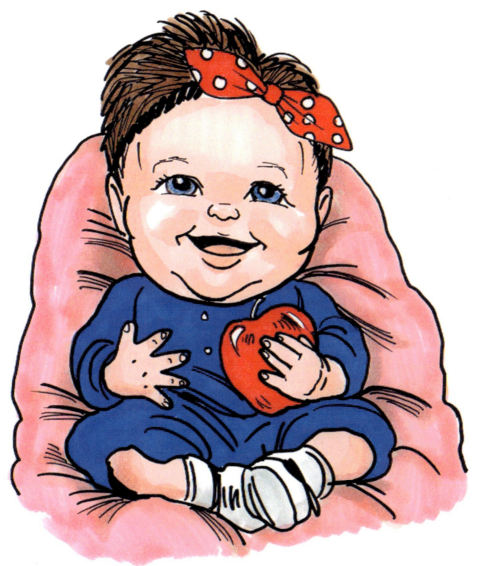

Zapple Apple Muffins

INGREDIENTS

- Combine in a bowl:
- 1 ½ cup firmly packed **brown sugar**
- ⅔ cup **oil**

- 1 **egg**
- 1 ½ cup **diced apples**
- 1 ½ cup **chopped pecans**

In another bowl combine:

- 1 cup **buttermilk**
- 1 tsp **Baking soda**

- 1 tsp **salt**
- 1 tsp **vanilla**

DIRECTIONS

1. Combine **sugar, oil,** and **egg** in a bowl.
2. Combine **buttermilk, baking soda**, **salt** and **vanilla** in another bowl.
3. Add milk mixture to **sugar** mixture alternately with 2 ½ cup of **flour.**
4. Mix well after each addition.
5. Fold in **apples** and **pecans**.
6. Pour into muffin papers (pans)
7. Sprinkle with ⅓ cup **sugar** combined with 1 tsp melted **butter.**

Bake at 325F for 30 minutes or until cake tester comes out clean.

Makes approximately 15 muffins.

Apple Pickin with Lil Mish

Lil Mish

Sweet Potato Muffcuits

INGREDIENTS

- ¾ cup mashed **sweet potatoes**
- 4 tsp **baking powder**
- 1 Tbls **sugar** or **honey**
- ⅔ cup milk

- ¼ cup oil
- 1¼ cup flour
- ½ tsp salt

DIRECTIONS

Preheat oven to 450F

1. Mix **potatoes, milk, oil,** and **honey** or **sugar** in a bowl combine remaining ingredients & add to **potato** mixture; dough should be soft

Cook batter in muffin tins about half full at 450F for 15 mins

Curious Cousins Isabella & Marcello

Auntie Laurie's Booberry Muffins

INGREDIENTS

- 2 eggs
- 2 cups flour
- ½ tsp salt
- 1 tsp vanilla
- ½ cup of softened butter

- 1 cup sugar
- 2 tsp baking powder
- ½ cup milk
- 2 ½ cup blueberries

DIRECTIONS

1. Mix butter, sugar, and add one egg at a time.
2. Add dry ingredients, alternately with milk and vanilla.
3. Crush ½ cup of blueberries and add to batter.
4. Stir the remaining blueberries into the bowl; try not to smash.
5. Sprinkle a little sugar on top of each.
6. Bake at 375F for 20-25 minutes.

Lovely Auntie Laurie

Auntie
Laurie

Grape Nut Bread

INGREDIENTS

- 1 cup **Grapenut cereal**
- 2 cups **buttermilk r**
- 3 ½ cups **flour**
- 2 tsp. **baking powder**

- 2 **eggs**
- 2 cups **suga**
- ½ tsp. **salt**
- 1 tsp. **baking soda**

DIRECTIONS

1. Soak **Grapenuts** in **buttermilk** for 10 mins.
2. Cream **sugar** & **eggs**
3. Add **milk** & **nuts** mixture
4. Stir in dry ingredients
5. Pour mixture into 2 loaf pans

Bake at 350F for 45 minutes or until toothpick is clean

Sous Chefs Mish & Stacey

Michele & Stacy

Lemony Bread

INGREDIENTS

- 2 **eggs**
- ⅓ cup **oil**
- 1½ cup **flour**
- 1 teaspoon **baking soda**
- ½ cup **nuts**

- 1 cup **sugar**
- 1 teaspoon grated **lemon** rind
- ½ teaspoon **salt**
- ½ cup **milk**

DIRECTIONS

1. Mix first 4 ingredients in a bowl.
2. Add dry ingredients, alternately with ½ cup of **milk**.
3. Mix in nuts. Bake in long pan at 350F for one hour.
4. Let stand in pan for 5 minutes. Remove; poke holes all over top of cake with toothpicks.

Mix ½ cup **sugar** and juice of one **lemon**; pour over cake.

Daring Cousin DENA

Cousin Dena

Cinnamon Hot Loaf

INGREDIENTS

- ¼ cup **sugar**
- ¼ cup **raisins**
- 1 roll of piping hot **Pillsbury loaf**
- 2 tsp **cinnamon**
- ¼ cup chopped **nuts**

DIRECTIONS

1. Grease cookie sheet.
2. Unroll **loaf** to form a sheet.
3. Sprinkle the **sugar** mixture roll up with slit sides up and seal.

Bake at 350F

Glaze: top of loaf with ½ cup **powdered sugar** and 2-3 teaspoons of **milk** combined together.

CINNAMON TOAST

INGREDIENTS

3 tablespoons **sugar**
1 teaspoon **cinnamon**
½ stick softened **butter**
4 slices whole **wheat bread**

DIRECTIONS

1. Measure **cinnamon** and **sugar** into a medium size bowl; Stir until well mixed. Toast **bread** in toaster remove and butter right away sprinkle with **cinnamon**

Good & Gooey Auntie Gina

A "CINNAMON" LOVES CINNAMON TOAST!

Auntie Gina

Life is good Miniature Pizza's

INGREDIENTS

Pre-heat oven to 350F

- 6 **English muffin** halves toasted (from toaster)
- 1 can (8oz) **tomato sauce**
- 1 cup grated **mozzarella cheese**
- ¼ cup **Parmesan cheese**
- **Salt, Pepper, Garlic salt**, and **Oregano**

DIRECTIONS

1. Using a small saucepan on top of the stove, heat up the
2. **Tomato sauce,** add **salt, pepper, garlic salt, oregano** and **Parmesan cheese** until it comes to a bubble.
3. Lower heat and simmer for 10 minutes. Turn off gas; Let cool.
4. Spoon 1-2 Tablespoons of the **tomatoes sauce** mixture on each toasted **English muffin**, add **Mozzarella cheese.**

Bake on cookie sheet at 350F for 20 minutes or until cheese bubbles.

Cool for 5 minutes and Serve.

Jovial Cousin Johnny

Cousin Johnny

Chicken and Rice Casserole with Corn Soufflé

INGREDIENTS

- 1 cup uncooked **rice**
- 1 cup **chicken** cut into cubes or strips
- ¼ lb **butter** (1 stick)
- 1 pkg. dry **onion soup mix**
- 4 cups boiling **water**
- **salt** and **pepper** depending on your taste

DIRECTIONS

Preheat oven at 350F

1. Grease bottom of 13x9 pan
2. Cover bottom of pan evenly with **rice**
3. Dot with **butter**
4. Add **chicken, soup mix, water, salt** & **pepper**

Bake for 1 hour

CORN SOUFFLÉ

INGREDIENTS boxes of *Jiffy Corn Bread*

- 2 cans of **creamed corn**
- 2 cans of **regular corn**
- 2 sticks of soft **butter**
- 2 **eggs**

DIRECTIONS

Preheat the oven to 350 F

1. Mix all the above ingredients together in a bowl.
2. Pour into a 9x13 round and Bake for 30 minutes.

Lusciously Delish Auntie Linda

Auntie Linda

Big Tuna Casserole

INGREDIENTS

- 2 cans **Tuna fish with spring water**
- 1 can **sweet peas** (or corn)
- 1 **can cream of mushroom soup**
- Some grated **cheddar cheese**

DIRECTIONS

1. Drain and flake a can of **Tuna fish.**
2. Put in the bottom of a casserole dish. Drain the **sweet corn** and layer on top of the tuna.
3. Pour the **mushroom soup** over the tuna and peas
4. Sprinkle **cheese** all over top of casserole.

Bake in a hot oven until warm.

Perfected by Cousin Pasquale

Pasquale

Children's Delight Beefy Casserole

INGREDIENTS

- 1 Pd of **Ground Beef**
- 1 can **Mushroom soup**
- 1 can **yellow corn**

- ½ pt. of **sour cream**
- 16 oz bag of **egg noodles**

DIRECTIONS

1. Brown the **ground beef** in a saucepan with a little salt and pepper. In a separate pan fill with water until boiling, add bag of **egg noodles** until done.
2. Mix **Mushroom soup**, **corn** and sour cream together in a bowl and add to casserole dish.
3. Bake at 350 F for 1 hour

Powered by Cousins Pat & Anthony

Cousin Pat & Cousin Anthony

Cheesie Mac

INGREDIENTS

- ½ cup (1 stick) **butter**, plus more for baking dish
- 1 lb. **elbow macaroni**
- ½ cup **flour**
- 5 cup **whole milk**
- 1 ½ tsp **Salt** and **Pepper**
- 1 tsp. **mustard powder**

- 1 c. **shredded cheddar**
- 1 c. **shredded Swiss**
- 1 ½ c. **grated Parmesan**, divided
- 1 c. plain **bread crumbs**
- 3 tbsp. extra-virgin **olive oil**
- Freshly chopped **parsley**, to garnish

DIRECTIONS

Preheat oven to 375°.

1. **Butter** a 9"-x-13" baking dish. In a large pot of salted, boiling water, cook **macaroni** until al dente. Drain and set aside.
2. In a large saucepan, melt 1 **stick butter**. Sprinkle over **flour** and cook until slightly golden, 2 to 3 minutes. Pour in **milk** and whisk until combined. Season with **mustard powder, salt, and pepper**.
3. Let simmer until starting to thicken, about 5 minutes.
4. Remove pan from heat and whisk in **cheddar, Gruyere**, and 1 cup **Parmesan**. Continue whisking until melted and smooth. Stir in cooked **macaroni** and transfer to prepared baking dish.
5. In a small bowl, combine remaining Parmesan with **bread crumbs** and **oil**. Sprinkle mixture over **macaroni**.

Bake until bubbly and golden, 25 to 30 minutes.

Garnish with parsley before serving. Let sit 10 minutes before serving.

Acquired for Cousin Ariana

Cousin Ariana

Hot Dog Spaghetti Casserole

INGREDIENTS

- 1 pound **spaghetti**
- 1 jar **spaghetti sauce**

- 1 package **hot dogs**, sliced into rounds
- **American Cheese** shredded

DIRECTIONS

Heat oven to 350 F degrees.

1. Cook **spaghetti** as directed on package; rinse and drain.
2. Butter a casserole dish or pan.
3. Layer **spaghetti, sauce, hot dog** slices, more sauce, and top with **shredded cheese**.

Bake about 30 minutes or until casserole is bubbly and the cheese is melted.

Creme de la creme Auntie Denise

Auntie Denise

Teriyaki Chicken Wings

INGREDIENTS

- ½ cup **soy sauce**
- ¾ cup **vinegar**
- 2–3 **garlic** cloves crushed
- 2 tablespoons **brown sugar**
- 3 pounds **chicken wings**

DIRECTIONS

Preheat oven to 375F.

1. Mix everything but the wings together. Place wings in large pan. Pour sauce over the **wings**, and bake until **wings** are done and golden brown.
2. Stir occasionally.

Mixing it up Uncle Michael

Uncle Michael

Rainbow Spaghetti

The most colorful way to eat spaghetti

INGREDIENTS

- 6 Ziploc bags
- 1 lb. spaghetti, cooked
- Food coloring (we used 6)
- 1 c. Water, Divided
- 3 tbsp. butter, melted
- ⅓ c. freshly grated Parmesan
- Dash Salt and Pepper

DIRECTIONS

1. Place 2 tbsp. water into each zip lock back (we used 6 for 6 different colors). Add 10 drops gel food coloring to each bag.
2. Divide the spaghetti into the 6 different bags. Shake until they are coated in their colors.
3. Remove pasta individually from zip lock bag and rinse with cold water. Combine in a large bowl and toss together with butter and parmesan.
4. Season with salt and pepper and serve.

Mastered for Johnny Carmine

Johnnie Carmine

Children's Easy Cobbler

INGREDIENTS

- 1 can refrigerated **buttermilk biscuits**
- 1 can (1 lb. 5oz) **pie filling**

- 1 pkg. lemon flavored **Jello** (3oz)

Topping

- ½ cup sifted **flour**
- ½ cup granulated **sugar**
- 1 can of either **cherry, peach** or **apple pie filling**

- ½ cup **margarine or butter**
- ¼ tsp. **salt**

DIRECTIONS

1. Combine **flour, sugar**, and **salt**
2. Cut in **margarine** until coarse and crumbling
3. **Butter** 9-inch square pan
4. Press separated **biscuits** to cover bottom of pan
5. Spread filling over dough, then sprinkle w/ the dry **jello** and cover with topping

Bake at 375F for 20-25 minutes

Grandiose Grandma Carol

Grandma Carol

Pudding Cookies

INGREDIENTS

- ¾ cup **Bisquick**
- ¼ cup **oil**
- 1 pkg. instant **pudding**
- 1 **egg**

DIRECTIONS

Heat oven at 350F
1. Mix all ingredients together until dough forms a ball
2. Shape into little balls using 1 tsp of dough for each
3. Flatten to about 2-inch sizes

Bake for 8 minutes; serves approx. 3 dozen

Holy Cannoli Cousin Nicoli

Cousin Nicoli

Chocolate Krispy Peanut Butter Balls

INGREDIENTS

- ½ cup butter or ½ cup margarine
- 2 cups chunky peanut butter
- 1teaspoon vanilla (optional)

- 1lb powdered sugar
- 3cups rice, krispies

DIRECTIONS

1. Melt butter and while hot, stir in peanut butter.
2. Mix well and add vanilla, powdered sugar and Rice Krispies.
3. Work in with hands until it will form balls.
4. If using paraffin shred on a box grater then add to the chocolate in a double boil and heat till melted and combined.
5. Dip into melted chocolate and paraffin or shortening with toothpick.

Cool on waxed paper.

CHOCOLATE DIPPING SAUCE

1. Melt in microwave 2 ounces paraffin wax or 2 ounces shortening
2. and 1 (24 oz) package chocolate chips

Chief Chef Mommy Cindy

Mom Cindy

Light as a Feather Cheese Cake

INGREDIENTS

- 1 pkg. lemon **Jello**
- ½ lb. **cream cheese**
- ½ cup **sugar**

- 1 can Eagle brand **condensed milk**
- 1 graham cracker **pie shell**
- 1 Tbs. **vanilla**

DIRECTIONS

1. Dissolve lemon **Jello** into 1 cup boiling water; let cool
2. Blend **cream cheese**, **sugar**, **vanilla** until smooth
3. Whip **condensed milk** with **jello** mixture until stiff
4. Fold Jello cheese mixture until well blended; do not beat
5. Pour in graham cracker **pie shell**; refrigerate and serve cold

Fancy & Flavorful Cousin Nicole

Nicole

Yum Yum Plum Baby Food Cake

INGREDIENTS

- 2 cups **self-rising flour**
- 2 cups **sugar**
- 1 cup **oil**
- 1 cup **nuts**

- 2 sm. jars of **plum filling**
- 1 tsp. **cinnamon**
- 1 tsp. **cloves**
- 3 **eggs**

DIRECTIONS

1. Mix all ingredients together
2. Place in greased tube pan

Bake at 325F for 1- 1½ hrs.

Yummy and Nummy Sista Angela

Flowerpot Sundaes

INGREDIENTS

- 1pint **vanilla ice cream**
- 1pint **strawberry ice cream**
- Multicolor tiny mints
- 8 (7 oz size) **paper cups**, in pretty colors or designs
- 8 (2- 2 ½ inch) **round lollipops**, in various colors
- 1 tube pink **frosting** with writing tip
- 4 spearmint **gumdrop** leaves, split in half
- Chocolate shot
- 1pt **pistachio ice cream**
- 8 **marshmallows**
- green **sugar crystals**

DIRECTIONS

1. With ice cream scoop, fill each paper cup with ¾ cup **ice cream**, using flavors desired. Place covered in freezer.
2. To make **lollipop** flowers as pictured; cut **marshmallows** with scissors around edge, to make petals. Attach a **marshmallow** "flower" to one side of lollipop with squirt of frosting.
3. Make rosette of frosting in center of **marshmallow** flower.
4. Attach **spearmint leaves**, one on each side of lollipop-stick stem, with dab of frosting. Insert flowers in **ice cream**.
5. Sprinkle **ice cream** with **green sugar crystals**, **multicolor mints**, or **chocolate shot**.

Scrumptiously Sista Alexandria

Alexandria

Fun with Knox Blox's

INGREDIENTS

- 2 pkgs. **unflavored gelatin**
- 1 6oz. pkg. **Jell-O**
- 2½ cups cold **water**
- ¼ cup **sugar**

DIRECTIONS

1. Dissolve **unflavored gelatin** in 1 cup cold water
2. Set aside in sauce pan
3. Boil 1 cup water
4. Add **Jell-O** & sugar; bring to boil
5. Remove from heat; add mixture and continuing stirring then add ½ cup cold water & continue stirring

Refrigerate & serve cold

CHOCOLATE KNOX BLOX

INGREDIENTS

- 4 envelopes **Knox gelatin**
- ½ cup **sugar**
- 1½ cups cold **water**
- 1 pkg. semisweet **chocolate pieces**

DIRECTIONS

1. Combine all ingredients in sauce pan
2. Stir constantly over low heat for 5 mins.
3. Pour into an 8x9 square pan; refrigerate until firm
4. Add **nuts, raisins** or **marshmallows** on top if desired

Funtastic by Chefs Santo & Vinci

Cousin Santo & Cousin Vinci

Mish's Yogurt Popsicles

INGREDIENTS

- 1 carton **yogurt**
- 16 oz concentrated **orange juice**

DIRECTIONS

1. Mix **yogurt** and **orange juice** together and freeze in molds

DEANNA'S FAVORITE FUDGYSICLES

INGREDIENTS

- 1 pkg **chocolate pudding**
- 3 ½ cups **skim milk**

DIRECTIONS

1. Prepare **pudding** as package directions require
2. Mix in **skim milk**
3. Freeze in molds

Delightful Cousin Deanna

Deanna

Marshmallow Popcorn Balls

INGREDIENTS

- 2 Tabl. **butter**
- ½ box of 3-oz **Raspberry Jell-O**
- 3 cups **Marshmallows**
- 3 qts unsalted **popped popcorn**

DIRECTIONS

1. In a saucepan melt **butter**, add **marshmallows** and stir until melted.
2. Blend in dry **Raspberry Jell-O** and mix well with buttered hands.
3. Form into balls, Cool and Enjoy!

Magnificent Marcello

Marcello

Refreshing Fruit Delite

INGREDIENTS

- 8 oz **cool whip**
- ¾ cups **sugar**
- 1 pt. frozen **strawberries**
- 1 can of drained **pineapple**

- 8oz **cream cheese**
- 2 **bananas**
- ½ cup of **crushed nuts**
- **Chocolate** cups

DIRECTIONS

1. Mix all ingredients together in a bowl
2. Freeze
3. Spoon out in **chocolate** cups

Serve cold

EASY PEZY JELLO

INGREDIENTS

- 1 small curd **cottage cheese**
- 1 cup **orange juice**
- 1 small **cool whip**

- 1 can **Mandarin oranges**
- 1 can **Pineapple chunks**

DIRECTIONS

1. Blend **cottage cheese**, **oranges** and **orange juice** and refrigerate until firm.
2. Remove from refrigerate and add can of **pineapple** and cool whip mix together with above ingredients and chill in refrigerator before serving.

Invented by Cousin Isabella

Isabella

Hercules's Simple Hot Cocoa

INGREDIENTS

- 1 ½ cups sweetened cocoa
- ½ teaspoon cinnamon
- ¼ teaspoon nutmeg
- 2 cups boiling water
- 3 cups milk
- 8 large marshmallows

DIRECTIONS

1. In large saucepan, combine cocoa, cinnamon, and nutmeg
2. Gradually stir in water, then milk
3. Heat carefully, stirring often (be careful not to scorch)
4. Serve cocoa hot, topped with marshmallows

Makes 8 servings

WARM MULLED CIDER
to warm up tummy!

INGREDIENTS

- 1 gallon cider
- ½ cup light brown sugar
- 8 inch cinnamon sticks
  (break into small pieces)
- 10-15 whole all spice
- 20-25 cloves

DIRECTIONS

1. In 6 qt kettle, bring all ingredients to boil, simmer uncovered approximately 30 mins
2. Strain through double layer of cheese cloth
3. Refrigerate cider till needed. Reheat for serving. Place a cinnamon stick stirrer in each mug (if desired)
4. Makes 12-15 serving

Spirited Cousin Sammy

Sammy

Banana-Nutella Smoothie

INGREDIENTS

- 1 cup **Nutella** spread
- ¼ cup creamy **peanut butter**
- 2 cups vanilla **yogurt**
- 1 ¼ to 1 ½ cups **soy milk**
- 4 medium **frozen bananas**

DIRECTIONS

1. Combine **Nutella, peanut butter, yogurt, soy milk** and **banana** in a blender. Process until smooth.
2. For thinner texture, add ¼ cup more soy milk and 3 or 4 ice cubes and process until ice is crushed. Pour into glasses.

Luscious Cousin Lauren

Cousin Lauren

Printed in the United States
by Baker & Taylor Publisher Services